D. The Rialto Bridge in Venice.

E. A carving of Noah, person from the bible, on the side of the Doge's Palace.

F. Boats are used as ambulances in Venice.

G. Coffee shops line the sides of the canals.

We acknowledge the financial support of the Government of Canada through the Book Publishing Industry Development Program (BPIDP) for our publishing activities.

A. *Boats are used as buses in Venice.*

B. *Tourists ride in gondolas beside the Doge's Palace.*

C. *Gondolas skim across the Grand Canal.*

ITALY
the land

Greg Nickles

A Bobbie Kalman Book

The Lands, Peoples, and Cultures Series

Crabtree Publishing Company

www.crabtreebooks.com

The Lands, Peoples, and Cultures Series

Created by Bobbie Kalman

Coordinating editor
Ellen Rodger

Production Coordinator
Rosie Gowsell

Project development, photo research, and design
First Folio Resource Group, Inc.
Erinn Banting
Pauline Beggs
Tom Dart
Bruce Krever
Debbie Smith

Editing
Maggie MacDonald

Separations and film
Embassy Graphics

Printer
Worzalla Publishing Company

Consultants
Patricia Bucciero, Embassy of Italy–Ottawa; Carlo Settembrini, Italian Cultural Institute

Photographs
Mary Altier: cover, p. 15 (bottom); Roberto M. Arakaki/International Stock: p. 9 (left); M. Bertinetti/ Photo Researchers: p. 5 (top); Wesley Bocxe/Photo Researchers: p. 29 (top right); Corbis/Neil Beer: p. 26 (bottom); Corbis/Jonathan Blair: p. 11 (left), p. 21 (right); Corbis/Jerry Braasch: p. 23 (right); Corbis/ Marcello Galandrini: p. 29 (bottom right); Corbis/ John Heseltine: p. 23 (left); Corbis/Maurizio Lanini: p. 10 (bottom); Corbis/David Lees: p. 8 (top); Corbis/ Tom Nebbia: p. 31 (top); Corbis/Richard T. Nowitz: p. 26 (top); Corbis/ Charles O'Rear: p. 28 (top); Corbis/Brian Pickering/ Eye Ubiquitous: p. 6; Corbis/Enzo & Paolo Ragazzini: p. 20 (bottom); Corbis/Hans Georg Roth: p. 25 (top); Corbis/Paul Thompson/Eye Ubiquitous: p. 10 (top); Corbis/Sandro Vannini: p. 7; Corbis/Felix Zaska: p. 24 (bottom); Peter Crabtree: front endpapers, back endpapers, title page, p. 4, p. 12 (both), p. 14 (top), p. 15 (top), p. 16, p. 18 (both), p. 19 (top), p. 21 (left), p. 22 (bottom), p. 25 (bottom), p. 27 (both), p. 30 (left), p. 31 (bottom); Mario De Biasi/Digital Stock: p. 17 (bottom), p. 20 (top); C. Falco/Science Source/Photo Researchers: p. 11 (right); James Foote/Photo Researchers: p. 22 (top); Georg Gerster/Photo Researchers: p. 9 (right); Jeff Greenberg/Archive Photos: p. 24 (top); Wolfgang Kaehler: p. 3; Richard T. Nowitz: p. 12 (top), p. 17 (top); G. E. Pakenham/ International Stock: p. 14 (bottom); R. Pharaoh/ International Stock: p. 29 (bottom left); Porterfield-Chickering/Photo Researchers: p. 30 (right); Reuters/ Archive Photos: p. 13 (bottom); Gianni Tortoli/ Science Source/Photo Researchers: p. 13 (top); Michael Ventura/ International Stock: p. 8 (bottom); Terry Whittaker/ Photo Researchers: p. 28 (bottom); Brian Yarvin/ Photo Researchers: p. 5 (bottom), p. 19 (bottom)

Map
Jim Chernishenko

Illustrations
Dianne Eastman: icon
David Wysotski, Allure Illustrations: back cover

Cover: The village of Vernazza crowds the rocky shore of Cinque Terre, a region in northern Italy.

Title page: Cars and buses negotiate the winding road that runs through a small, hilly town in the Ligurian mountains of northwestern Italy.

Icon: Olive trees, which produce one of Italy's most important crops, appear at the head of each section.

Back cover: The golden eagle lives in the Alps, a mountain range in the north of Italy.

Published by
Crabtree Publishing Company

PMB 16A
350 Fifth Avenue
Suite 3308
New York
NY 10118

612 Welland Avenue
St. Catharines
Ontario, Canada
L2M 5V6

73 Lime Walk
Headington
Oxford OX3 7AD
United Kingdom

Cataloging-in-Publication Data
Nickles, Greg, 1969–
Italy, the land / Greg Nickles
p. cm. -- (The lands, peoples, and cultures series)
Includes index.
ISBN 0-7787-9369-9 (RLB) -- ISBN 0-7787-9737-6 (pbk.)
1. Italy--Description and travel--Juvenile literature
[1. Italy.] I. Title. II. Series.
DG430.2.N53 2001
945--dc21

LC 00-057073
LC

Contents

An ancient land

For thousands of years, people have lived in Italy's mountainous countryside, along its sunny coasts, and in its **fertile** valleys. Most cities founded in ancient times still stand today. They are filled with buildings of long ago. Some are in ruins and some are almost perfectly preserved. The largest and best-known city, Rome, is the country's busy capital.

For most of Italy's history, each region had its own rulers. It was only in 1861 that the country was united under one government. Since then, Italy has grown into a wealthy industrial nation.

The old city of Florence. From left to right, the brown city hall tower, the small dome of the baptistery, the tall bell tower and the Duomo, or Cathedral of Florence.

Facts at a glance

Official name: Repubblica Italiana (Italian Republic)

Area: 116,314 square miles (301,252 square kilometers)

Population: 57.5 million

Capital city: Rome

Official language: Italian

Main religion: Roman Catholicism

Currency: the lira and euro

National holiday: June 2

(above) Ancient ruins, like the Temple of Antonius and Faustina, stand alongside modern buildings in Rome.

(below) Apartment buildings painted in white, yellow, orange, and red are perched on a cliff overlooking the port in Manarola, in northwestern Italy.

From north to south

Italy is a peninsula, a long, narrow strip of land that looks like a boot jutting into the Mediterranean Sea. About three-quarters of the land is made up of mountains and hills. The snowy Alps are in Italy's north. The rolling Apennines run down the center of the country.

Italy's mountainous areas are so dry and rough that very few people live there. Most of the country's farms, towns, and cities are crowded into a few flat regions such as the large Po Valley and along parts of the coast.

Up in the Alps

In the far north of Italy, the Alps tower above the land. These jagged, snowcapped mountains form a natural boundary between Italy and its neighbors, France, Switzerland, Austria, and Slovenia. Along the border with France stands Italy's highest peak, Monte Bianco, at 15,771 feet (4,807 meters). The Matterhorn, a horn-shaped peak that is a favorite of mountain climbers, is on the border between Italy and Switzerland.

(opposite page, right)
The Dolomites, a mountain range in the northern Alps, loom high above a forest and a rushing river.

(opposite page, bottom)
Fertile farmland stretches out from the shores of Lake Bolsena, in central Italy.

Dense forests and grassy meadows cover the Alps' steep mountain slopes. Some farmers use the slopes as pasture for their herds. Others grow grape vines there. Cold, clear lakes, including Lakes Maggiore, Como, and Garda, are also found among these mountains. The lake beds were carved out by glaciers. These enormous sheets of ice crept across the land thousands of years ago. Today, only a few small glaciers are found high in the mountains.

The Apennines

The Apennine mountain chain divides most of Italy into western and eastern halves. These mountains are not as tall or steep as the Alps, but they are very rough. The tallest peak, Monte Corno, stands 9,560 feet (2,914 meters) high.

The Apennines are mostly dry, except for a few lakes. Lakes Bracciano, Nemi, and Bolsena are actually in the craters of extinct volcanoes. Not all the Apennine volcanoes are extinct! Sometimes there are eruptions at Mount Vesuvius, not far from the coastal city of Naples.

Down in the lowlands

Most Italians live in the lowlands, the flat regions that border the rivers and seas. The majority of Italy's farms and industries are also found there because the lowlands' soil is very fertile. The flat land also makes it easy to transport goods from place to place.

The Po Valley

The Po Valley, between the Alps and the Apennines, is Italy's largest and most-populated lowland region. Water from the Alps' melting snowcaps flows down streams and rivers into this valley and the Po River. The Po River runs the length of the Po Valley on its way to the Adriatic Sea. Another river, the Tiber, flows through Italy's other main lowland region. This region lies along the western part of the country, near Rome.

A long coastline

Italy's long coastline stretches almost all the way around the country. Much of the shore is rocky, but there are also many sandy beaches. Italy's sunny shores have long been a favorite holiday destination for tourists. Today, the Italian Riviera, an area along the country's northwest shore, is an especially popular vacation spot for people from all over the world.

Three farmers work in their fields beside the Po River near Cremona, in northern Italy.

Italians relax and enjoy the warm weather at a beach on the Italian Riviera.

Italy's islands

Italy includes about 70 islands in the Mediterranean Sea. The largest are Sicily and Sardinia. Sicily sits about ten miles (sixteen kilometers) from the mainland's southern tip. It is very mountainous. Most Sicilians live along the coast because much of their island's interior is too rough to settle. There are many earthquakes and volcanic eruptions, including those of Europe's tallest active volcano, Mount Etna.

Sardinia is smaller and further from the mainland than Sicily. Some of its land is mountainous and more than half is covered with pastures. Sardinia is especially popular with visitors who come to enjoy its white sand beaches and 3,000-year-old rock structures, called *nuraghi*. Traces of more than 7,000 of these small, cone-shaped structures can be seen today.

Mount Etna towers above the ruins of the ancient Taormina Theater on the island of Sicily.

St. Peter's Square stands at the center of Vatican City in Rome.

Tiny countries

Italy has two tiny, independent countries — San Marino and Vatican City — within its borders. San Marino sits on the slopes of Mount Titano, near Italy's east coast. First settled in the fourth century, it is only about eight miles (thirteen kilometers) wide and has just over 20,000 citizens. Its major industries include tourism, agriculture, and **handicrafts**. Fine printing, especially of postage stamps, is also an important source of income for the country.

Vatican City is even smaller than San Marino. It sits within the city of Rome. Just a few blocks in size, it is the center of Roman Catholicism, a **denomination** of Christianity. Christianity is a religion based on the teachings of Jesus Christ, who many believe was the son of God on earth. The pope, the head of the Roman Catholic Church, and about 1,000 other leaders of the Church live in Vatican City.

Earth, wind, and fire

Italy is not a large country, but it has many kinds of weather. The climate is different in the mountains than in the lowlands and parts of the country are affected by natural disasters such as earthquakes, landslides, and volcanic eruptions.

A Mediterranean climate

The weather in most of central and southern Italy and on Italy's islands is very warm and dry. Summers are hot and little rain falls. Winter days are often so mild that people still swim in the warm sea. Unfortunately, this weather often leads to drought, long periods of dryness which make it difficult to grow crops.

Alpine winters

Summers in the Alps are short and cool, and winters are long and bitterly cold. During Alpine winters, the snow falls very heavily — in some places up to 30 feet (9 meters) each year! Although the Alps have very cool weather year-round, they keep lands to the south warm. They act as a shield, blocking the strong wintry winds that blow south from central Europe.

People relax on a sunny day in the Piazza della Rotunda in Rome.

Snow blankets a village in the Alps.

Wild winds

Many strong winds whip through Italy. Two are the *bora* and the *scirocco*. The *bora* blows from the northeast, where Italy meets Slovenia, during winter. It is very cold and very strong. Sometimes, it even knocks people down and overturns cars! The *scirocco* blows from the south or southeast in the summer and is very warm. It comes from dry North Africa, where it picks up sand. Then, it travels across the Mediterranean Sea, where it picks up moisture. When the *scirocco* reaches Italy, it is wet and brings fog or rain. It also dumps sand on the land.

Two people read on the flooded patio of a café in Venice.

From the depths of the earth

Italy's wild winds seem tame when compared to the destruction caused by volcanoes. Two of Italy's largest volcanoes are Vesuvius, in the southern mainland, and Etna, on the island of Sicily. Usually, the volcanoes just smolder, but on occasion they explode, spewing ash and fiery **lava** on the surrounding countryside. Stromboli, Italy's third major volcano, is located in the Tyrrhenian Sea. Over thousands of years, the lava from this volcano, which flows constantly, has formed the small island of Stromboli.

Italy's volcanoes have erupted many times over the centuries, destroying homes and killing many people. Recently, **engineers** have tried "taming" the eruptions by using ditches, walls, and explosives to direct lava away from nearby houses and villages.

Pompeii's disaster

In 79 A.D., Mount Vesuvius exploded after centuries of being inactive. People in the nearby city of Pompeii were caught by surprise as their homes and streets were buried under more than nine feet (three meters) of volcanic ash and mud. The disaster destroyed Pompeii and the towns surrounding it, killing thousands of people.

Unearthing the ruins

Centuries passed before the ruins of Pompeii were uncovered. In 1748, **archaeologists** began to excavate, or unearth, its buildings. They found the city well preserved under layers of volcanic ash. As they dug, excavators also found holes in the ash where Pompeii's citizens died. Over hundreds of years, the ash hardened around people's bodies. By pouring plaster into the holes, the excavators made **casts** of the victims.

Today, Pompeii is an important place to learn about life in ancient times. In 1997, it was recognized as a World Heritage Site, a label given by the United Nations Educational, Scientific, and Cultural Organization (UNESCO) to protect historical treasures.

The volcano Vesuvius covered this Pompeii street with ash for more than 1700 years. Archaeologists found a well preserved city beneath the layers of ash and soil.

The plaster cast of a body found in the ruins of Pompeii lies in a display case surrounded by other artifacts discovered at the site.

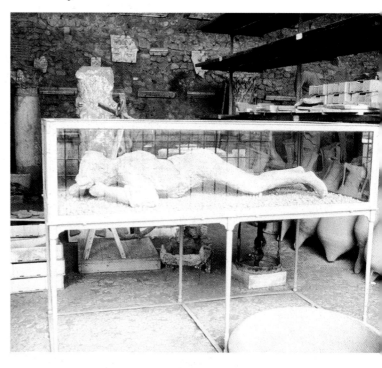

Deadly earthquakes

When Italy's volcanoes erupt, they often cause violent earthquakes. Earthquakes also happen when huge amounts of lava, gases, or rock shift deep underground. Many Italian villages, towns, and cities are threatened by earthquakes. In 1980, an earthquake in Naples killed 4,500 people, while one there in 1805 took more than 65,000 lives.

Disastrous landslides

The mountainous parts of Italy's south have frequent landslides. They are caused by earthquakes and rain, which shift the soil on the steep slopes. Dirt, mud, and debris come crashing down the hillsides, taking with them trees and even houses. Roads are blocked and homes are destroyed by these disasters.

(right) An apartment building's front doors and part of its walls are all that remain after an earthquake near Naples.

(below) A man shovels mud away from the front of a house after a flood on the western coast.

The Italians

Italians come from many backgrounds. Most people are **descendants** of ancient Romans who once ruled the region. People from other parts of Europe, North Africa, Asia, and the Middle East have also settled on the land.

Regions and treasured traditions

Before Italy became a united country in 1861, people in each region had their own customs, traditions, and dialects, or versions of Italian. Today, people in each region still have their own traditions and still speak the local language with their family. However, they usually use **standard Italian** outside the home. Some Italians also speak completely different languages such as the French-Italians who live near the border with France and Switzerland and the Slavic-Italians who live near Slovenia.

(right) A woman in the northern Alps rakes grass and places it in a basket on her back.

(top) A group of friends gather at a busy outdoor market in Milan in northern Italy.

14

A girl helps her mother carry home groceries for a family dinner. They moved to Italy from the Dominican Republic in the Caribbean.

A fishmonger displays his fish at a market in Venice. He uses the scale on the table to weigh a customer's purchase and determine the price.

Recently arrived

In the last 50 years, thousands of people from other countries have settled in Italy. Some, such as North Africans, Asians, and people from the Middle East, came in search of jobs in Italy's growing industries. Others, especially from the nearby parts of the former Yugoslavia, came fleeing war. Most immigrants have settled in Italy's large cities, especially in Rome, Milan, Turin, and Genoa.

Italians abroad

Several countries in Europe and around the world, including the United States, Canada, Argentina, and Brazil, have large Italian populations. Poverty was common in Italy in the late 1800s, especially in the southern countryside. Millions of people began **emigrating** from Italy in search of better lives. When their families in Italy saw how much better life was overseas, they followed.

Another wave of emigration followed World War II (1939–1945). People moved to other countries that had not been damaged by the war, as Italy was. Today, emigration from Italy has slowed to a trickle because jobs are plentiful in a prosperous Italy.

Rome, the Eternal City

Rome is Italy's capital as well as a center of business, arts, and industry. Its history stretches back thousands of years, earning it the nickname "the Eternal City."

Visitors to Rome are astounded by its many impressive buildings, monuments, and works of art. Along its wide avenues and narrow, winding streets stand great churches and ancient ruins. Large squares are decorated with beautiful fountains and statues created by some of the world's most famous artists. Busy Romans travel through their noisy streets in cars, on scooters, on bicycles, and by foot. Many others relax in the city's countless parks, theaters, and cafés.

The Forum was built over 900 years during the time of the Roman Empire. This center of trade, politics, and religion included cathedrals, government buildings, and statues.

Ancient Romans

Rome was founded about 2,700 years ago on the banks of the Tiber River. It began as a collection of forts built on seven hills. Over the next thousand years, the Romans took over Italy and the surrounding lands. They built one of the largest and richest **empires** in history. In the centuries after its empire crumbled, Rome became the center of the powerful Roman Catholic Church.

Echoes of the Empire

Today, signs of Rome's past can be seen everywhere. In the center of the city, called the Ancient City, stand the remains of fortress walls and the Forum, where the empire's government once met. Another famous ruin is the 2,000-year-old Colosseum. There, crowds once gathered to watch gladiators, or slaves who fought one another or wild animals to the death. Other buildings of the past are well preserved, such as the Pantheon, a domed temple completed around 126 A.D.

Signs of Christianity

Vatican City and Rome are important centers of Christian worship. Vatican City is home to St. Peter's Basilica, one of the world's largest churches. Rome is filled with over 500 churches as well as other buildings constructed by the Church. The Quirinal Palace, for example, was built 500 years ago as a home for the pope. Italy's president now lives there. Christian history is also found underground. Visitors can still wander through the catacombs, which are tunnels and rooms built under the city. Early Christians hid in the catacombs from those trying to **persecute** them because of their religious beliefs.

Fountains and *piazzas*

Rome is filled with fountains and *piazzas*, or squares. They were built by some of Italy's greatest artists at the command of powerful popes and other rulers. Today, people gather around them to relax, meet friends, and enjoy the weather. One of the most popular fountains is the Fontana della Barcaccia, at the foot of the wide, curving Spanish Steps. From the church at the top of these steps, visitors can enjoy the view of Rome below. At the famous Trevi Fountain, visitors toss coins over their shoulder into the water. It is said that this custom will ensure their return to Rome.

The Colosseum could hold up to 55,000 spectators at a time.

People gather on the Spanish Steps which overlook the Piazza di Spagna, in the center of Rome.

17

Splendid cities

Italy's beautiful cities were founded in ancient times. Today, they bustle with business, industry, and millions of tourists who come to see the historic buildings and works of art.

Florence, city of art

The northern city of Florence sits among rolling hills. It was a fortress during the time of the ancient Roman Empire, then later grew and became home to some of the world's most famous artists and scholars. From the 1300s through the 1500s, the period known as the *Rinascimento* or Renaissance, these artists and scholars worked for rich Florentine families. Their art and ideas inspired great new works throughout Europe.

(left) The Piazza or square of San Marco in Venice in front of the Basilica, or Cathedral of St. Mark.

(below) The medieval walled town of Siena, with its Piazza del Campo, or town square with the city hall tower.

The Ponte Vecchio was built during the 1300s. Today, shops that sell gold and silver line the famous bridge.

Modern-day Florence

Culture is still an important part of Florence. Florentine artists are known for their fine work in glass, metal, silk, lace, and leather. People visit **artisans**' shops along the Ponte Vecchio, one of the city's oldest bridges. They also flock to the streets and *piazzas* of the city's old downtown, where some of the finest churches and palaces built during the Renaissance still stand. The fortress-like Palazzo Vecchio, or "Old Palace," once home to the city's rulers, and the domed Santa Maria del Fiore Cathedral are two of the most famous attractions.

Stylish Milan

Milan is Italy's business center. It is home to many of the country's largest manufacturers, including the giant Pirelli rubber company. It is also the country's fashion capital. Twice a year, designers from around the world show their latest creations at Milan's fashion shows.

There are more than 3,000 sculptures on the exterior of Milan's **duomo.**

In Milan, the new buildings that house the city's big businesses are surrounded by many older buildings. One of the most striking is the Milan *duomo* in the city center. This huge marble cathedral took over 500 years to build. It was finally completed in 1897. It is decorated with 135 tall, pointed **spires**, many of which are capped by sculptures of people. Another impressive building is La Scala, which has been Milan's opera house since 1778. La Scala is often called the world's best opera house.

Boats dock at the busy Santa Lucia port in Naples.

Ancient Naples

Naples is the largest seaport in southern Italy. It was founded around 600 B.C. Now, ancient castles stand side by side with modern apartment buildings. The oldest castle is the Castel dell'Ovo, or "Castle of the Egg," named after the oval shape of its walls.

Naples' industries include **textiles**, machinery, and chemical production. However, the city is best known as the home of one of the world's favorite foods — pizza. Pizza is said to have been invented there in the 1700s.

Modern Turin

Turin is a modern-looking city. Many of its old buildings were destroyed during World War II. In the years since, Turin has been rebuilt with new apartments, office towers, and factories. Several large companies, such as the car manufacturers Fiat and Lancia, are based there.

Turin's cathedral of San Giovanni Battista is home to a mysterious cloth called the Shroud of Turin. On it is printed the figure of a dead man. No one knows where the shroud came from, how the print was made, or who the man was. Some people said it was Jesus Christ. They believed that the shroud was used to wrap his body after he died. In 1988, however, scientists proved that the cloth was created about 700 years ago, more than 1,200 years after Christ's death. Still, many people consider the Shroud of Turin a symbol of Christianity.

Cars, trucks, and buses crowd the streets of Turin during rush hour.

Palermo, Sicily's port

Palermo, the capital of the island of Sicily, is a major port city. Although some parts sit in ruins from World War II, many historic buildings survive. Each of the city's former rulers, including the Romans, North Africans, Germans, French, and Spanish, constructed buildings in different styles. For example, the Palatine Chapel of the Royal Palace was completed in 1189 by North Africans. They decorated this house of worship with patterned carvings, paintings, and mosaics, or tile work, that were popular in North Africa at the time.

Venice, the City of Canals

Venice is a beautiful city built on about 120 islands in the middle of a **lagoon**. The old part of the city has canals instead of streets and there are no cars or trucks. People travel from place to place in boats or on foot across the 400 bridges that span these waterways. Many of the canals are very narrow and run like alleys between buildings. The main waterway, called the Grand Canal, is 225 feet (70 meters) wide. It curves through the city center. Each day, it is crowded with passenger boats of all sizes.

Laundry hangs from lines that stretch from balcony to balcony across Palermo's busy city streets.

Past, present, and future

Venice was built about 1,600 years ago. It grew into a rich city 1,000 years ago when it became an international center for trading and shipping. The city has changed little since then. Most of its buildings, including its palaces and churches, are at least 600 years old. They include the luxurious Palace of the Doge, which once housed Venice's rulers, and the San Marco Basilica, which is decorated with golden mosaics.

Today, Venice remains a major port, but tourism has become its largest industry. Each year, millions of people come to see its beautiful buildings and ride along the canals. Venetians are concerned, however, because their city is sinking very slowly into the seabed. Engineers are trying to figure out how to fix the **foundations** of the city's buildings and the ground below them so that they do not sink further.

A gondolier navigates a narrow canal in Venice.

Crops and livestock

Millions of small, family-owned farms throughout Italy grow crops and raise **livestock**. The main crops are the same ones that have been grown in the country for centuries: tomatoes, grapes, lemons, oranges, olives, and grains such as wheat and rice.

Farming difficult land

The Po Valley, in the north, is Italy's most fertile region. It is difficult to grow crops in the rest of the country. The mountains and hills are steep, their climate is either too hot and dry or too cool, and the soil is rocky. Farmers have several strategies to make use of this rugged land. Some cut terraces, which look like steps, into the hills, making flat areas on which to grow crops. Others use the grassy slopes as grazing land for livestock.

Favorite fruit

Italy's sunny climate is ideal for growing different kinds of fruit, including lemons, limes, kiwis, and oranges. Some of the largest harvests are of tomatoes and grapes. Tomatoes were introduced to Europe from Mexico about 500 years ago. At first, people thought they were poisonous. By the 1800s, however, cooked tomatoes had become a favorite pasta sauce. Today, Italy's exports of fresh and canned tomatoes are a huge source of income. Grapes, which have been farmed for centuries in fields and on steep slopes, are grown for Italy's large wine industry.

Olive trees and vineyards cover the hills of Tuscany. The grapes from these vineyards will be used to make Italy's famous chianti wine.

Huge barrels are filled with tomato paste at a factory in Naples.

Harvesters wrap huge mesh nets around the base of olive trees so that they can gather any olives that fall on the ground.

Olives and their oil

Olives are one of Italy's favorite foods and most valuable crops. Green and black olives, both large and small, are served on their own, used in other foods, or pressed for their oil. Olive trees thrive in the dry, stony regions in southern Italy, in Sardinia, and in Sicily. The trees have been known to live for hundreds and even thousands of years. Their fruit take six to eight months to grow and are harvested between November and March. Some farmers use machines to shake the olives from the trees, but many still pick their crop by hand.

Freshly picked olives spoil very quickly. They must be shipped to a mill within a day. There, many are preserved in brine, or salt water, for eating. Other olives are crushed into a paste between revolving steel **grindstones**. The paste is mixed with water and then placed in a large press, which squeezes out the olive oil.

The product of this first pressing is given the name "extra virgin olive oil," meaning it is of the highest quality. The **pulp** may be pressed again to make "virgin" oil or heated with chemicals to draw out the lowest quality oil, which is called "pure."

From grains to pasta

Grain crops, especially rice, wheat, and corn, are a main part of the Italian diet. Rice is grown in parts of the Po Valley that are flooded to create large paddies, or rice fields. Wheat and corn are grown in the drier south. Durum wheat is the most popular variety grown in Italy. Its hard grains are ground to make semolina, the main ingredient in pasta, a favorite Italian food. Corn is ground into cornmeal and boiled with water to make polenta. Polenta is eaten as a porridge or served toasted or fried in northern Italy.

Raising livestock

Italian farmers raise many sorts of livestock. Pork, beef, and veal are favorite meats produced in the north. Cattle are also raised for milk. Sheep and goats are raised on dairy farms in the south, in Sicily, and in Sardinia. Their milk is used to make different kinds of cheese. Water buffalo are raised in Sicily and in the southern part of the mainland. Their milk is used to make mozzarella cheese.

It will take a while for this farmer to milk all the goats by hand.

Industrial Italy

Farming has always been an important part of Italy's economy, but in the last 50 years more and more factories have been built. Today, Italy is one of the largest manufacturers of machinery, chemicals, electronics, cars, and trucks. Though there are some large companies in Italy, the vast majority are owned by families and employ less than ten people.

Italy has built up its industries and trade by closely cooperating with its neighbors. After World War II, Italy joined an organization that today is known as the European Union (EU). The EU encourages its members to trade goods with one another. In 1999, the EU introduced the euro, a new **currency** used by all its member countries. The euro makes trade between countries easier.

(right) Lamborghinis are some of the fastest cars in the world. They can exceed speeds of 185 miles per hour (298 kilometers per hour).

(below) Huge containers filled with cargo wait to be loaded onto ships at the port in Salerno, in southern Italy.

The automakers

Some of the world's fastest and best-selling cars are designed and built in Italy. Fiat sells more cars that any other company in Europe. It was founded a century ago by Gianni Agnelli. It grew after World War II from sales of its small, affordable cars. Alfa Romeo and Ferrari, two brands of sports cars, are also owned by Fiat. Other famous Italian sports cars include Lamborghinis and Maseratis.

Slabs of marble are each marked with a number. The marble will be used for buildings and artwork around the world.

Carrara's white marble

The town of Carrara, near the northwest coast, is known around the world for its marble industry. The mountains surrounding Carrara are made of white marble that sculptors and builders have used for the last 2,000 years. Workers use explosives and cables to cut the mountainsides into slab after giant slab of marble. After each slab topples to the ground, it is cut into smaller blocks and slowly hauled away by trucks along roads that snake dangerously through the mine.

Quality and style

Italy has a reputation for manufacturing high-quality, stylish products. For centuries, skilled artisans have made everything from violins and hand-stitched lace to furniture and fine jewelry. Sometimes, the artisans of a particular town or village specialize in one craft. For example, the city of Venice has been home to master glass blowers for a thousand years. Towns such as Vicenza and Arezzo are famous for their goldsmiths, or people who make crafts out of gold. Even products made in factories, such as household appliances, are known for their good quality and interesting design.

Popular fashion

Italy's strong sense of design can also be seen in the country's fashion industry. Expensive leather shoes, wallets, and purses are a specialty of Italian leatherworkers. Fine Italian textiles have been admired for centuries, as have the skills of the country's spinners, weavers, and sewers. Rome and Milan, both world capitals of fashion design, have been home to famous Italian designers such as Valentino, Versace, and Armani.

Two shopowners stand outside their boutique, which sells stylish purses and shoes in Sestri Levante.

Getting around

There are many ways to travel around Italy. Each day, millions of people speed across the country on highways, high-speed trains, and planes. Local travelers take buses and streetcars, or get around on their bicycles and scooters.

Roman roads

Italy's first paved roads were constructed by the Romans about 2,000 years ago. These roads were made in ways similar to ours — with a solid bed of sand or gravel and a smoothly paved surface. The Romans did not have bulldozers or steamrollers to help them. Instead, they had to construct their roads by hand, with the help of simple tools. Paved with tightly fitted stones, the roads were built so that people traveled them for centuries afterward.

(right) Many ancient roads, like the Appian Way in Rome, are still in use today.

(below) A streetcar drops off and picks up passengers on the via Grossi in Milan.

Highways and rails

Italians love automobiles. Highways and city streets are always packed with cars! To avoid traffic jams, people in the city take buses, streetcars, and sometimes the *metro*, or subway. Very fast passenger trains, called *espressos* or *rapidos*, are also popular. They run across the countryside between major cities. For local trips, people ride the slower *accellerato* trains.

A difficult landscape

It is difficult and expensive to construct roads and rail lines through the mountainous regions in Italy. To cross the many peaks and valleys, Italian engineers designed special bridges and long tunnels. The Simplon tunnel, for example, is over twelve miles (nineteen kilometers) long. It runs through the Alps between Italy and Switzerland.

Boating in Venice

In Venice, where there are canals instead of streets, people rely on boats for daily travel. The most common boats are motorized *vaporettos*, which taxi many people at once. The traditional boat of the canals, however, is the long, flat-bottomed **gondola**. Gondolas seat only a few people and are steered by a gondolier. The gondolier pushes the boat through the water with a special oar called a sweep. Thousands of gondolas once packed Venice's canals. Today, only a small number of these remain for tourists and for special occasions such as weddings. Gondolas may be decorated with flowers to take the bride to church.

(above) In Venice, gondolas are used to carry passengers from place to place and to transport goods, such as fruit and vegetables, to shops.

(left) A woman tries a new type of scooter at a car show in Milan. The bar on top helps prevent riders from getting injured in accidents.

 # Wild plants and animals

Many wildlife species, such as wolves, brown bears, and lynx, were once common in Italy. They are now scarce because of thousands of years of hunting and **logging**, which destroyed their homes. Today, wild plants and animals survive mainly in the country's remote mountains and surrounding seas.

The source of cork

Pine, olive, cypress, and laurel trees are all common in Italy. One of the country's most interesting trees is the cork oak, which grows in the Alps and in the mountains of the south. The spongy bark of these trees is used to make bottle corks. A cork oak's bark is harvested by hand once the tree is 25 years old. Harvesters strip off the rough outer bark to expose the spongy inner layer, which is then carefully pried away. If stripped carefully, the trees survive to produce another layer of cork every few years.

(top) Harvesters use axes to carefully cut away sections of bark on a cork oak tree.

A golden eagle's diet consists mainly of small animals such as rabbits, rodents, and snakes.

The great golden eagle

Golden eagles soar high above Italy's forests and mountain slopes. These birds, named for the golden feathers along the back of their neck, have a large wingspan of about 8 feet (2.5 meters). They nest on treetops or in caves on cliffs. From high in the sky, they use their sharp eyesight to pinpoint prey on the ground. These great birds, the symbol of the ancient Roman Empire, were once plentiful in Italy. Today, few survive in the country.

Swordfish and sharks

The warm sea waters surrounding Italy are full of colorful wildlife. Sponges and red corals are found close to shore. Farther out, fish such as tuna, dentex, and red mullet swim. Smaller fish are prey for the 15-foot (4.5-meter) swordfish, which is named after its long, pointy nose. Scientists believe that swordfish use their nose to slash at prey. The Mediterranean Sea is also home to the white shark. These sharks can grow up to 36 feet (11 meters) long. They will eat anything, even ships' garbage, to satisfy their enormous hunger. They have also been known to attack swimmers and boaters.

Furry marmots

Far below the soaring eagles, marmots scurry across Italy's mountain slopes and plains. Marmots are very large **rodents** that grow up to 2 feet (60 centimeters) long, plus a tail of up to 10 inches (25 centimeters)! They live in underground burrows in large groups called colonies. While hunting for green plants and farmers' crops to eat, marmots often stand on their back legs to look for danger. If they spot an enemy, they whistle to warn other marmots.

The male moufflon uses its huge horns to attract mates and to defend itself from danger.

Pig cousins

Packs of wild boars — the larger, wild cousins of pigs found on farms — roam through many of Italy's forests. Wild boars come out in the evening and snuffle along the ground, digging up whatever food they can find with their sharp tusks. While they are usually calm, the dark, bristly haired boars are known for their ferocity, strength, and speed when angered.

(right) Wild boars eat both plants and animals such as reptiles and birds.

(below) A marmot peeks out from beneath a rock in the Alps.

A changing environment

Many Italians use bicycles instead of cars.
This helps lessen air pollution.

Like other countries, Italy is facing many environmental challenges. Some of these problems have developed over centuries. Others are more recent. They are the result of pollution from modern factories, homes, and automobiles.

Centuries in the making

For thousands of years, people have cut down Italy's forests, drained marshes, and plowed the land. These activities became more common in the last hundred years as new factories and homes were built in the countryside. As a result of the loss of these natural lands, much of the wildlife that lived there is gone.

Shifting soil

Clearing forests has also led to landslides. When trees are chopped down from a hillside, they no longer protect it from rain and their roots cannot hold the soil together. Flooding or earthquakes then cause loose soil to tumble down the hills. As a result, many mountain slopes are stony and bare. **Soil erosion** also happens on flat land such as farmers' fields. Soil with nutrients that used to hold crops is carried away by the wind or washed by rain into nearby streams and rivers.

Pollution in the air

Air pollution is another problem. It is caused by exhaust, a poisonous smoke, from the country's factories, energy plants, and motor vehicles. Many cities are sometimes covered with smog, a fog of smoke and chemicals. This leads to breathing problems and other illnesses. Poisons in the air also hurt Italy's priceless marble buildings and sculptures. They make the surface of the marble soft, so that it gradually washes away in the rain.

Pollution destroys many beautiful frescoes,
or paintings, on the walls of buildings
throughout Italy.

Poisonous waters

Italians also worry about water pollution. There are many causes of water pollution. Chemicals in the air mix with the rain and fall to the earth. Poisonous waste from factories and homes flows into the seas. Fertilizers seep from farmers' fields into rivers. Water pollution ruins Italians' drinking water and destroys the beauty of the seaside. In Venice, the problem of sinking buildings is made worse by chemicals in the water that eat away at the buildings' foundations.

Cleaning up

In recent years, Italians have worked to clean up their environment. To cut air pollution, they have begun using cleaner energy sources. Energy plants that run on **solar power**, **methane** gas, and even vegetable oil have been built as experiments to replace dirty coal- and oil-burning plants.

The government is also trying to decrease the number of cars on the roads. Commuters are encouraged to take streetcars and electric trains. Many cities have banned cars from downtown sections on certain days and, in some cases, permanently. These efforts have been partly successful, and Italians continue to look for new ways to solve their country's pollution problems.

Garbage, including plastic bottles and paper, washes up by a dock on a canal in Venice.

Workers restore the walls of an ancient building in Assisi. The walls crumbled because of pollution.

Glossary

archaeologist A person who studies the past by looking at buildings and artifacts

artisan A skilled craftsperson

cast A plaster mold used to preserve artifacts

currency Money

denomination A religious group within a faith

descendant A person who can trace his or her family roots to a certain family or group

emigrate To leave one country for another

empire A group of countries or territories having the same ruler or government

engineer A person who uses science to design and build structures and machines

fertile Able to produce abundant crops or vegetation

foundation The part of a building that supports it

gondola A long, flat-bottomed boat used in the canals of Venice

grindstone A flat, round stone turned by a crank that is used to crush food and sharpen tools

handicraft A craft made by hand

lagoon A shallow body of water connected to a large body of water

lava Molten rock that flows from a volcano

livestock Farm animals

logging The cutting down of trees in a forest

methane A colorless, odorless, and flammable gas

persecute To harm another person for religious, racial, or political reasons

pulp The soft part of a fruit

rodent A small animal with sharp teeth that are used for gnawing

soil erosion The loss of soil due to wind and rain

solar power Electricity generated from sunlight

spire The tall, pointed top of a tower

standard Italian The version of Italian that is most commonly spoken and written outside the home

textile A fabric or cloth

Index

1 2 3 4 5 6 7 8 9 0 Printed in the USA 0 9 8 7 6 5 4 3 2 1

The marvelous city of Florence.

A. *The statue of a pope looks down from the duomo.*

B. *The huge duomo, or cathedral, in Florence was built 600 years ago in the fourteenth century. It took almost 100 years to complete.*

C. *The tall front door of the duomo.*

D. *Two friends sit on a wall above Florence. The duomo's large, red dome is in the distance.*

A. This eight-sided building is the baptistry where children are baptised into the Roman Catholic Church. It was built 1,000 years ago.

B. Students rest beside the statue of Grand Duke Cosimo I, one of the old rulers of Florence.

C. Italian students walk through the Palace of the Uffizi, which was built by Cosimo I. It now houses many famous Italian paintings. The tall building in the background is the Palazzo Vecchio, Florence's city hall.

D. Two students sit beneath a statue of Boccaccio, who in 1350, wrote the Decameron, a book of stories about Italian life.